APRIL AT THE RUINS

Books by Lawrence Raab

Poetry

*April at the Ruins*
*The Life Beside This One*
*Mistaking Each Other for Ghosts*
*A Cup of Water Turns into a Rose* (chapbook)
*The History of Forgetting*
*Visible Signs: New and Selected Poems*
*The Probable World*
*Winter at the Caspian Sea* (chapbook with Stephen Dunn)
*What We Don't Know About Each Other*
*Other Children*
*The Collector of Cold Weather*
*Mysteries of the Horizon*

**Essays**

*Why Don't We Say What We Mean?*

# APRIL AT THE RUINS

POEMS

LAWRENCE RAAB

TUPELO PRESS
North Adams, Massachussetts

Library of Congress Cataloging-in-Publication Data
Names: Raab, Lawrence, 1946– , author.
Title: April at the Ruins: poems / Lawrence Raab.
Description: North Adams, Massachusetts : Tupelo Press, 2022.
Identifiers: LCCN 2021054308 | ISBN 9781946482655 (paperback)
Classification: LCC PS3568.A2 A87 2022 | DDC 811/.54–dc23/eng/20211213
LC record available at https://lccn.loc.gov/2021054308

Cover art: Cezanne, Paul (1839-1906). "Blue Landscape," c1903.
Found in the collection of the State Hermitage, St Petersburg, Russia
Photo Credit : HIP / Art Resource, NY

Cover and text designed by Bill Kuch.
First paperback edition April 2022

Acknowledgments:
*The American Journal of Poetry*: "Pleasures of a Minor God," "Perhaps," "One of Those
Secret Lives," "In America" (as "Moment by Moment") and "A Little Music."
*Hampden-Sydney Poetry Review*: "Lost" and "The Awful Pleasures." *Plume*:
"A Children's Story" (*Plume Poetry #7*), "'The World Provides Evidence for Almost
Anything'" (*Plume* online), and "April at the Ruins" (as "Late Spring," *Plume Poetry #8*).
*Solstice*: "Swan Song." *Two Hawks Quarterly*: "Stopping by Woods." *Under
a Warm Green Linden*: "My Expedition," "Twilight," and "In the Earliest Days."
*Volume*: "Pastoral," "Why We Are Here," "After the Sky Had Fallen," and "Just
Now." A different version of "Until Evening" appeared in *The Life Beside This
One* (Tupelo, 2017). The basic story of "One of Those Secret Lives" is taken from
Nathaniel Hawthorne's "Wakefield." Finally, many thanks to Williams College
for continuing to support my work. –L.R.

Tupelo Press
P.O. Box 1767
North Adams, Massachusetts 01247
(413) 664-9611 / Fax: (413) 664-9711
editor@tupelopress.org / www.tupelopress.org

Tupelo Press is an award-winning independent literary press that publishes fine fiction,
non-fiction, and poetry in books that are a joy to hold as well as read. Tupelo Press is a
registered 501(c)(3) non-profit organization, and we rely on public support to carry out
our mission of publishing extraordinary work that may be outside the realm of the large
commercial publishers. Financial donations are welcome and are tax deductible.

This project is supported in part by an award
from the National Endowment for the Arts

For Katie and Molly and Lucy

without whom
many poems would not have been written

# CONTENTS

...those obstinate questionings
Of sense and outward things,
Fallings from us, vanishings...

those first affections,
Those shadowy recollections,
Which, be they what they may...
Are yet a master light of all our seeing.

—William Wordsworth
"Intimations of Immortality"

APRIL AT THE RUINS

1

## LOST

Wherever it is, it will never ask
for your attention,
unlike the click of a door,
the scent of lilacs,

or the distant barking of a dog.
Easy enough to overlook
in the general disarray,
you might still notice its shadow

passing through a wavy pane
of glass, and be reminded
of one of the rooms
of childhood—an open window

and a desk, then a picture
of someone too far away
to make out, as if nothing
here really wanted to be seen again.

This is why what's lost
stays lost, and can never
be only the actual
letter, or knife, or ring of keys

you've been trying
so hard all day to find.

# IN THE EARLIEST DAYS

death and chance
were brothers, and suffering
didn't turn anyone

into a better person.
What happened happened.
The sun vanished

and returned.
For a while everybody
was more afraid than usual.

Perhaps this was a sign.
But of what?
No one had yet learned how

to wonder about such things.
All of the world
was only itself. So the night

must have been magnificent
in its loneliness, and the dawn
a kind of rapture we can't imagine.

# AFTER THE SKY HAD FALLEN

At the beginning: a foolish mistake.

At the end the fox eats them all.
After which the thatch
of night surrounds

the lost children, who sometimes
find their way home
and sometimes do not,

while the stars turn into maps
which is how
the wise men were guided.

They set their gifts
in the straw before the manger,
and stepped back.

One of them thought:
*But what use can the child have
for such things?*

Yet the firelight loved
those treasures, and would not
leave them alone

until they found their place
in the story. Meanwhile,
the children walk deeper

into the forest. *Surely*
*God will help us,* the boy
tells this sister. *No,*

she replies, *the world*
*has abandoned us.*
Whereupon an old woman

steps out of the shadowy trees.
*Dear ones,* she exclaims,
*how thin you are!*

*Come to my cottage*
*and I will give you pancakes*
*and apples.* Of course

the children follow her
because they cannot see
she is a terrible witch

who plans to cook them
in the morning, and eat them
for supper. But that night

she tucks them gently
into bed, and kisses them
just as their mother had.

Or else: a snow-white bird
watches those children
sleeping in the cold forest

and is touched
by their dreams, and sings
so sweet a song that when

the children wake they believe
this music will guide them
through the great maze of trees

until they arrive at a meadow
where they will look up
to see the familiar stars

and not far away a little house
so much like home
they cannot help

but think: *Surely*
*we will be happy now.*

# FALSE DAWN

The monasteries were closed;
the monks who remained
lit candles to pretend
the darkness wasn't permanent.
And some were troubled
in the false dawn—
had loving God
become too difficult?
Silence enfolded them.
In this way they were like us
as we lie in bed, sleepless,
watching the headlights of cars
slide across the ceiling, remembering
when we took our lives for granted.
The monks had been taught
to welcome death.
What was there to lose except
the body and its troublesome
secrets and needs?
They lit their candles because
they always had,
and because repetition
is a comfort, the shape of a day
falling into place
as if it belonged to us.

# PERHAPS

So there you are
on the porch of the house by the lake
where your father and mother
sit in that autumnal haze

your dreams frequently require.
And you're a boy, of course,
gazing across the water, waiting

for your real life to begin,
although you haven't tried
to invite it any closer.

How alone you were, how much
like your father.
Which you didn't understand.

*What else couldn't you see?*
a voice in your dream
demands. *Think about it.*
So you get up, make coffee,

watch the fog drifting
as it does in the movies
through unconvincing graveyards

and bleak English moors
and now the field beyond your lawn.
Your father is out there
in the tall grass, smoking a cigarette.

He's been dead for a long time,
but he's still reluctant
to talk. You could suggest

a few words—he might admit
that when he was alive
he also woke early, and made coffee,

and stared out his kitchen window
at the houses of his neighbors,
their windows dark,

their secrets, like his, intact.
*And then*, he says, *I may have felt
the way you feel this morning.
But I didn't think about it.*

*Should I have thought about it?*
He knows that *yes*
is the answer you want.

*Yes*, he says, *perhaps
I should have thought
about everything
more often. Perhaps I did.*

*Now you tell me—
what difference would that have made?*

# A LITTLE MUSIC

*for Stephen Dunn*

Then it seemed that all of the poems
about death had been written.
And all of the poems about the future
had finally exhausted us
with the truth of their lamentations.
What is left for me now? the poet asks,
still hoping to give someone
the chance to walk out into a meadow
of improbable beauty.
Or through the streets of an ancient city,
the windows open, the murmur
of voices mixing
with the murmur of the sea.
This is the moment
the poem wants to leave us with—
the men and women
of that place
lying in each other's arms
as sleep offers them
its consolations, and a little music
arrives from far away.

# A CHILDREN'S STORY

1

A man was walking in the rain
when he found a dog.
He took the dog home.
The dog was glad to be out of the rain.

The man gave the dog a bowl of water
and the dog fell asleep by the fire.
Then a boy knocked on the door
and asked the man if he'd seen his dog.

"No," said the man. The boy started to cry.
"OK," the man said, "I have your dog,
but right now the dog is sleeping.
Why don't you wait for a while?"

"No," said the boy. "It's late,
and I have to go home."

2

The man stood on his porch,
watching them leave.
He wasn't sure how to feel.
A bird flew down

and perched on the railing.
"Listen to me," the bird said,
"that boy just tricked you.
His dog isn't really his dog."

The man found the boy
and took the dog.
The boy began to cry. The man said,
"You're not going to fool me this time."


3


On the way home, a wolf
came out of the woods. The wolf said,
"That bird was lying to you."
"Why would a bird do that?" asked the man.

"Nature is all deception,"
replied the wolf. "Look at me.
I'm not going to eat you.
I just came to tell you the truth."

The wolf headed back
into the woods, and the man
and the dog went home.
The dog fell asleep by the fire.


4


But the man kept wondering:
Who should I believe? What should I do?
"Pay attention to me," said the fire.
"Everything I touch I have to destroy."

"What kind of answer is that?" asked the man.
But the fire had said all it wanted to say.
Then the dog woke up,
and went over to the man

and sat down beside him.
Look at me, the dog said without speaking.
Look at me and I will help you understand.
The man stared into the dog's eyes.

You will never know, the dog said,
to whom I belong.

2

# MY EXPEDITION

And so the ashen moon and the cold stars
burned on the lake beyond
the glow of our fire. *Soon*, I thought.

We had come too far to fail,

hacking through the jagged thickets
while all around us the forest
grew older and closer until
I was warned that no one

had ventured past
this black lake and its stillness.

Then a branch snapped, the air
shuddered, and she
whom I sought

was near me and watching.

What proof, after all,
does certainty require?

My companions were afraid,
demanding that we leave,
insisting I would never survive
if I stayed. Yet how badly

I wanted to press on,

to feel each day more determined,
more confident my hopes
would be rewarded.

Those who set out before me,
and turned back, have spoken
of the same disappointments.

Sometimes a haunting cry
from among the ancient trees
is added to their tales. Yet everything
they said they saw I had seen already.

And most of it was nothing

but heavy branches
adrift in the firelight, and a voice
almost like my own, urging me

to acknowledge the purpose
of my expedition—
that it had always been

to desire you, my love,

then travel this far
to discover
how to leave you behind.

# PASTORAL

That summer, just outside the city of Z——,
I couldn't decide
between ending my marriage to S.
or challenging R. to a duel.
Oh, I was aware
of what they were up to.
But I let things go, as we often do
in the face of difficulty.
Soon it was autumn,
season of endings. Bells were tolling,
which had once meant more
than the slipping of one hour
into the next. I took out my journal
and wrote a few sentences
on the subject of how easily
we are beguiled
by the appearance of things.
I must have felt like a philosopher,
which, as a student,
had been one of my ambitions
until my life with S. began
and everything around us seemed
always to be inviting us
effortlessly into the next moment.
So we wandered
through the many small but exquisite parks
for which Z—— is well known,
pausing at the fountains,
watching day dissolve into evening,
listening to the bells calling out
to whoever might have been
naïve enough to take them to heart.

# THE MINOR CHARACTERS

I went along with the idea
because I was supposed to,
and because Werner kept insisting
we finally had the science

to change the past, although Emily,
with whom I was in love,
said it would never work
and she was right. Delusions

of grandeur, she concluded.
But I understood how impossible
it would be for Werner
to give in to failure. Meanwhile,

those of us inclined toward caution
drifted through the lab,
checking the luminous dials,
maybe brushing up against

each other, maybe wondering
what to say next.
When I told Emily I loved her,
she stared at me, shocked

and angry—even betrayed.
Someone else should have said
what I said. Then everything
was over: the control panels

flickering and abuzz,
black smoke pouring
from the ventilators, flames
crawling up the walls.

Soon Werner will be trapped
beneath the crashing towers
of equipment, crying out
against Nature and God

and the blindness of men,
while the rest of us
fall out of the picture, our lives
that brief and incomplete,

because what's important
is happening elsewhere,
and was never
meant to include us.

# THE WEIRD MUSEUM

*Los Angeles, 1995*

The voodoo masks were fine,
the inspectors said, but the bodies had to go:
our 3,600-year-old Egyptian mummy,
our authentic Vlad the Impaler,
and all three of the severed heads.
"Human remains," they told us,
"must be properly disposed of."
I call it history. I say it's a crime
to throw Vlad away, who was, after all,
the real Dracula. You look at him
and picture the terrible things he did.
But times were different: he saved his people.
And then you think—maybe not so different.
Of course I can't prove it's Vlad,
and I have to admit the severed heads
could be in better shape: Hermander,
Henri Landru, and the last victim
of the Mad Butcher of Kingsbury Run.
This is a small museum, we don't have the money
to do it right. They told George he could keep
his Tarot readings, and I could sell my herbs
and oils, but we can't get by on that.
People want to see strange things.
And the dead? My feeling is
they don't mind being in a museum,
having people pay to look at them, think back
for a minute, remember who they were.

## YOU NEVER ACTUALLY DIE
## WHEN YOU DIE IN A DREAM

Deep in the woods something is always
ready to pounce. Which is why I prefer
a short walk around my cottage,
even if at any moment a crazy man

might stumble out of the bushes
and fix me with his fiery stare, demanding
that I face the truth about sin
and retribution, and how punishment

precedes the crime that deserves it,
but not always. This is wonderful!
I cry. Your ideas are the same as mine!
And he lets me go, dismayed

his vision isn't his alone, then alarmed
by my neighbor's dog
howling at the end of her chain
like a true prophet:

*How can you live the way you live!*
*How can you stand it?*

I'm not saying this happens every day,
but even the most questionable
revelation confirms my suspicion
that I'll never be released

from waiting deep in the woods
for something that knows me
to find me—something savage
and sane, like a wolf,

but as cruel as a man,
staring into my eyes, judging
my character,
convinced of my guilt.

## MOON AND SUN

There's a bargain between
the moon and the sun.

I won't say any more.

If I did I'd have to lie,
and I want you to trust me.
We've seen the sun mocking us

with its gaudy splendor,
and the moon, aloof and alone,
incapable of sympathy.

Why shouldn't we also
choose indifference?
Nothing out there cares for us.

Isn't that the sorrow of it?

Not to be cared for, not to be
again like a child.

# A LONG TRAIN RIDE TO THE SEA

No sooner had I departed
from the city
than I started wondering
about my destination.
Would the house I returned to
so often in my sleep
still be there in its whispery
grove of pines
not far from the sea?
The train pressed forward
into the landscape of my youth—
those burnished fields,
that vast, enigmatic sky.
Night began. Stars
floated by. The black trees
beside the rails looked
like emblems and I recalled
how sure I'd been
as a boy that the pale face
of the moon, or the hush
of evening, would reveal
what was being kept from me.
I knew concealment
led to recognition.
As we passed the glimmering
lights of towns, my reflection
in the window trembled,
then vanished,
then reappeared. Occasionally

the whistle of the train suggested
we were about to arrive
at someone's destination,
if not yet mine.

# DEATH OF THE INVISIBLE MAN

At the end he often returned
to the amazement
of watching himself disappear.
*An invisible man,*

he'd boasted to the air,
*can go wherever he chooses,*
*have anything that pleases him,*
*have anyone he desires.*

He shuttered the lab
and stepped into the night,
perfectly alone. *Soon,*
he told himself, *the world*

*will know me.* Above him
a window opened. A woman
leaned out—she'd heard
some noise in the street.

A candle wavered
in her hand. Shadows
touched her face.
*How tender,* he thought.

He never doubted
he had the skill to reverse
his transformation,
become a man like any other.

Nothing worked.
He grew careless,
was pursued, surrounded,
forced to submit.

In the weakness of his dying,
he barely whispered.
Yet if a glass
slowly rose above his bed,

then flew at the feet of those
who watched over him,
they felt his anger:
he was still there.

But to himself
he was hardly present.
*If I were to walk out*
*of this room*, he thought,

*rain would fall through me.*
*Windows would refuse*
*to contain my reflection. Cold*
*would pass me by.*

At the beginning
he'd been certain he would
never tire of the invisible,
and of the way

it set him apart
from the rest—the ones
who could so easily be seen,

and touch each other,
as he wished now to be touched.

# THE AWFUL PLEASURES

This much we all agreed was true: how we'd traveled
from the anvil of the west under the hammer of the sun,
while the risks each day grew more personal,
more demanding, stranger. Bewilderment
followed us through the gullies and the breaks.

The plains turned into stone, then snow.
And the wind tried to persuade us we should rest,
that the journey was endless and unimportant.
But afterward, so many praised
our bravery in ways that heartened us

we wanted to speak of the awful
pleasures of letting go, of falling
through the cold into sleep, welcoming
its touch. Yet we tried to remain committed
to our task, collecting everything we could find,

then kill, then pick apart to observe
what we held in our hands. Darling, forgive me
for my absence. We were fools
until we thought we were heroes.
There was too much to see.

Later I'll tell you of the marvels,
if I can recall why those storms and chasms
astonished us as they did. Often, I confess,
what came to me in delirium
was clearer than the truth. Even the way

I dreamt of you, and of how you held me,
and said my name—even that could have been
someone else whispering in my ear
about what I didn't know I'd given up
to become what I had become.

3

# THE SAINT IN THE PAINTING

keeps a skull on his desk
as a symbol of the end
of illusion, and the peace
that follows,
while in the many brilliant

and savage paintings
of that time, martyrs
destined to become saints
seem to welcome the arrows
embedded in their chests,

or the flames gathering
at their feet, or the knives
peeling the skin from their bodies.
In the museum of great masters,
I wish I were more surprised

by how many kinds of pain
those artists, or the priests
who paid them, decided
we needed to see. So I too
might have envied

the burning man's refusal
to believe fire
can take anything real
from him. His eyes
are lifted above the taunts

and jeers of the crowd,
his gaze fixed on the endless
unyielding sky. But in time
when loss promises
to overwhelm me

as it will, or I'm seduced
by the serenity
of that saint observing
the skull on his desk,
I pray that someone

I love will convince me
we must cling to this world—
even as it resists us, torments
and amazes us—
every day for the rest of our lives.

## PLEASURES OF A MINOR GOD

How carefully light picks through
the things of the afternoon,
saving that for later, moving this
out of its shadow: blade of a knife,
crumpled sheet of paper,

silver chain, all of it washed clean
of significance, unless some god
like myself, still enamored
of the idea of revelation, has chosen
to hide a few clues around your yard.

Like a toy some child abandoned,
certain he'd never want it back,
though he would. Or this picture
I've left beneath the purple asters
by the rickety fence—a face

blurred by weather, the size
of a locket on a delicate chain
near somebody's heart.
You can tell yourself you weren't
the one to discard it. But suppose

the light is a better judge
of what you should see, and why.
Or I am, having assembled all this.
That's how a minor god
amuses himself—arranging

toys, fiddling with wildflowers—
since no one offers me
incense these days, or prayers,
who once would have honored me
and been afraid.

Now I can only distress you
a little, compel you to kneel,
pick up a photograph, and pause:
When was it lost, why has it returned?
How much should you be ashamed?

Such poor pleasures as these
are all that's left of the work
that used to be mine.
I suppose you could say I'm
paying you back for leaving me

alone with a bunch of trinkets
I've quickly grown tired of,
as I've grown tired of you,
and your life, even the parts
I invented. Everyone's predictable,

clinging to what's gone. Which is true
for me as well. Diminishment
is the idea I should have ignored
to remain the god I was. Like a child
who doesn't know he has to change.

# JUST NOW

Who decided death was a good idea?
That lying in the ground in a box
is the right kind of ending?

*More life* is what I want.
But not surrounded
by all these quarrels

and deceptions
and crippling desires.
The world after this one

should have nothing in it
to covet or envy. Nothing
for time to disfigure,

rip apart, take away.
Therefore: no time.
Which leaves stillness

everywhere. I saw it then—
the boredom of clouds
and soft music, until someone

just sitting around remembers
a small treasure he hadn't
been allowed to bring with him,

since everything particular
is real, and therefore
impossible to save.

Like a favorite hat.
Or a bracelet. Or that colorful
wisp of a scarf you were wearing

the afternoon we met in the park.
I said something
about the sky. You pointed

to the light shimmering
through the tall pines as we
were leaving, and I

touched your hand
as if by accident.
As if I had changed my mind

about the future. Look,
you said, turning back
to see what was gone—

how lucky
we are to have been here
just now.

# THE BEAUTIFUL AFTERNOON OF CHANCE

*Alas! The onion you are eating is someone else's water lily.*
                                    —found in a fortune cookie


The tree you are watching is someone else's piano.
Or his horse, or the horse of his neighbor.
A friend you had almost forgotten

will soon arrive from a great distance.
Let the table be set for the marvelous lunch.
Your luck has changed completely.

But you should make more time to be surprised.
Tell somebody who is standing alone
the next thought that enters your mind.

Frequently the unexpected will reward you.
Frequently it will not.
Then let the joyful dishes appear—

the onions like water lilies, the chestnuts
like horses, or music, or snow.
Nothing is beyond repair.

Give a kiss to the one sitting beside you.
How can there be a beautiful ending
without many beautiful mistakes?

# WHY WE ARE HERE

*I don't know why we are here, but I'm pretty sure*
*that it is not in order to enjoy ourselves.*
—Ludwig Wittgenstein


One afternoon in Vienna
almost by chance you find yourself
in front of the house where Wittgenstein
once lived and considered
the difficulties of knowing what we know.

That was the summer you needed
to decide about love—whether or not
you were confusing it with affection.
Soon her train would arrive,
and she would step out onto

the platform, smiling but anxious.
So what sense does it make
that Saint Francis has followed her
into your thoughts? As a young man
he chose a life of pleasure.

Then he found God, gave everything
he owned to the poor,
and was loved by the animals.
Which is why in many paintings
he comforts a rabbit, or a mouse,

and why the birds flock to him
to be blessed. But now, as you hurry
toward the station, Saint Francis
turns into Venus, serenely
poised on her shell above the waves.

What happiness Botticelli must have felt
to have created her luxurious hair!
And all the rest of her splendid body.
Naturally he loved her, emerging
as she had from the labors of his art.

Perhaps he hoped to be loved in return.
Once hadn't such things been possible?
So you reach the station just as she steps
from the train, her long hair brushed
by the tenderness of the light of Vienna.

And you're struck—this is like
the beginning of a movie in which
a man and a woman meet on a train,
fall in, then out of love, then rob
a bank with such clumsiness

they must want to be shot, and he is,
but she doesn't care—not anymore—
since not caring, she tells him, is all
you get in this life to protect yourself.
"Well, that was depressing," your companion

remarks as the credits roll and the lights rise.
"We should have gone dancing.
Because if we aren't here to enjoy ourselves,
why are we here?" And she adds,
"You must realize, my friend, my sweet,

my little mouse, the world cares for you
as much as I do, which right now isn't much."
Such cruelty, however, could be the fault
of a poor translation from the French,
since this conversation is happening inside

a film inside that other film about theft
and betrayal and aimless disillusionment,
all of it arranged to make the point that art
is artifice, and must be different from,
or else the same as, what's real. Therefore,

when the woman you've come to meet
crosses the platform with that endearing
skip and shrug—why not tell her
you love her? And that seeing her
now in this station is like arriving

at the end of a long and perplexing story,
full of apparently meaningless
digressions that fall into place
in the final chapter, leaving the reader
astonished, and overwhelmed.

## ONE OF THE WAYS
## WE TALK TO EACH OTHER

It's not important, he said,
and she said, Tell me anyway.
But he didn't want to be told
what to do, so he said, That's why
I won't tell you, which he knew
didn't make sense. In that case,
she replied, I'm not
going to tell you either.
They went outside with the dog
where it seemed that being silent
wasn't the same as refusal.
I'm not quiet because I'm angry,
he thought, assuming she felt the same,
but she didn't. The dog sniffed
at a tuft of grass, tugged
on the leash. How can I begin
a new conversation? he wondered.
And she—well, her mind
had drifted off. But whatever
occurred to her next
pleased her, and as they crossed
the street she took his hand,
just as if everything
they hadn't told each other
had never happened.

## WHAT WE DID YESTERDAY

We woke later than usual.
Opened the shades, looked out
at the lawn. We wrote

to friends who needed
to be told that our dog,
Lucy, had died the day before.

In the afternoon we drove
to the store and waited while
the groceries we'd ordered

were carried out to the car,
since the virus had reached us,
and this was one of the ways

we could try to be safe.
At home we washed
our hands and started

picking up her toys,
water bowls, beds, some
to discard, some to give away,

a few—her collar,
her blue rabbit—to leave
where they were for a while.

Toward evening we took a walk,
keeping our distance, as required,
from the people we passed.

You said we were fortunate
the end had been sudden.
Yesterday morning—only

yesterday?—she was so weak
we could see she'd never
be herself again. The look

in her eyes was like my father's
when he was dying. It said:
*Something terribly wrong*

*is happening inside me,*
*which is why I must concentrate*
*only on that.*

We carried her downstairs
and made the arrangements.
The first injection

put her to sleep, the second
stopped her heart.
We stroked her gently

as though she could feel
our touch. I wanted
to cry but didn't. And then

we went home. Isolation,
we'd been told, is crucial
to flatten the curve, slowing

the progress of the virus,
which might mean
thousands wouldn't die.

But we should expect
to be alone
much longer than predicted.

To stay in the house. To leave only
if we needed to accomplish
some necessary task.

# LITTLE RITUAL

*Let that go, but keep this.*
                    —Tao Te Ching


The lake was a mirror.
I picked up a stone, broke the surface,
watched the sky return.

Another stone, a better one,
I saved and forgot. Later,
when I found it, all of its light

had drained away—
those zigzags of blue,
that shiver of quartz,

one morning
by the lake, just watching,
then picking up a stone

to keep track of where I'd been.
I didn't think about an end
to this collecting, didn't see

myself living in a house
so full of the past I'd never
escape being reminded

that some day everything
I love must be set aside,
or given away, or lost.

# FOR US

*On our 50th wedding anniversary*


Remember the song Jenny made up
that morning years ago beside the sea?
Everybody knows, she sang,
when the old days come. And so
they have. All our pictures
show us what looks like the past,
which doesn't mean
it hasn't changed.
Was the afternoon blue?
But we hadn't met that afternoon.
We were only about to meet.
Today we're astonished
fifty years have gathered
behind us, and we're grateful
so many friends
can be astonished with us.
But let's also remember,
my love, what was ours alone:
that winter when our breath
turned into stars
on the clear glass, though we
were warm enough, and our cottage
beside the woods where the rooks
quarreled like old married couples,
and once, perhaps twice, the owl
surprised us, gliding flawlessly
through the twilight. Later: violets
knitted through a field. Later still:

the aimless puff of a cloud.
Sometimes we felt we were
where we were meant to be.
But I'm certain I'm here
only because you're here with me.
Was that particular afternoon
gray, or no color at all, because
we hadn't yet met?
Then we did,
and the story of our lives
began without a plot.
That was the adventure.
Not knowing.
That was the satisfaction.
And now, my dear, what a joy
it is to look back and see us
when we were strangers,
and then the day after—reckless,
and unafraid, and in love,
just one step into the future.

4

# THE MUSE EXPLAINS

How hard it is, my lonely boy,
for you without me. How jealous
you become when you picture
someone new whose solitude
I've quietly entered, so much

like a lover. Like one who wishes
not to speak to be heard.
Now that I've left you, *fickle*
is hard to avoid, *unfaithful*
as well. But those words

belong to anybody,
and they will disappoint you
more than I have. Try to worry
a little about this. Also:
Don't wait for me.

I've never actually
whispered sweetly in anyone's ear,
or floated around with a harp,
dressed up in some gauzy outfit
I wouldn't in a million years

have chosen for myself.
In fact, I come and go
without a fuss.
You'd hardly notice me
if we passed on the street,

and we have. But I'm patient.
I can wait for you to hear
what I don't want to say.
What if I stood even closer?
If I always only listened?

## STOPPING BY WOODS

Imagine you're out there also
in the snow, not far from those trees
that seem to be hiding something.
Maybe you're concerned

that another traveler, even this late,
might see you and stop, and ask
why you stopped, if you're having
some kind of trouble.

What would you say,
what would you keep to yourself?
A few minutes ago
you weren't uneasy. Now you are,

and maybe there's a reason,
maybe there isn't.
But this is a poem.
It's not life, where nothing

has to add up. Which is why
you expect you'll be given
at the end some useful idea
about duty or time

to take home and ponder.
Yet the snow has disguised
so much, you're not sure
how long you should wait.

And you're tired—aren't you?—
watching the snow, lovely
as it is, falling,
and continuing to fall.

# ONE OF THOSE SECRET LIVES

Perhaps he had one of those secret lives
you read about, which means
he didn't die, but needed
to be someone else without me.
Of course I've asked myself

what I might have noticed—
a certain kind of moodiness,
or a fear that now we were
those people we would always be.
Or a different fear.

I see him kissing me goodbye,
the door half-open, the sky
half-covered by the usual clouds,
a jar of daisies on the end-table.
If everything is a clue, nothing is.

Death is the most important way
of being gone, but there are other ways.
Sometimes you get used to them.
For the first few weeks
I thought I could change things—

closing a window without looking
outside, going into the garden,
then quickly coming back,
as if the smallest adjustment
might persuade time to reconsider

what it had done. I suppose I didn't
expect that magic to work.
Or else I never tried hard enough.
After a while I gave up my sorrow,
stopped wondering who he might be with,

and how far away. Then I thought:
Maybe not so far away, but alone
and across the street, watching our house,
absorbed by what he still mistook
for grief. Even sharing it. As if this

made us husband and wife again.
Who can say what the heart
is capable of? One evening
he could be walking down this street
in the rain that is almost snow.

He'll be cold, and without thinking
he'll arrive at our door,
and turn the knob, and step inside,
expecting, perhaps, that I'll help him
take his coat off, and hang it up

beside the fire to dry. And I might do that,
because how can I know how I might feel?

# TWILIGHT

That morning, leafing through Aristotle,
I came upon: "For the things we have to learn
before we can do them, we learn by doing them."
I wondered if this was a reliable edition.

My wife Carol would have an opinion,
but she was asleep. I went outside
to rake leaves with Ralph from next door,
and mentioned the idea. "Yes," said Ralph,

"that's what I've always thought."
"I didn't realize you'd read Aristotle."
"I haven't, but that doesn't mean
what he says isn't what I feel in my soul."

Maybe Ralph was in love again,
and happy. Or at least content.
He went back to his house for lunch.
I watched a few leaves unfasten themselves

from the maples and descend to the lawn.
Later, Carol and I took our usual walk
through the park. We passed a bed
of roses. "Look at them," Carol said,

"those narcissists—still showing off
as if it were summer, and they were new."
Perhaps she was joking. "Maybe,"
I told her, "you could learn

to like them just by liking them."
"Maybe," she said, "I could do
something like that, as once or twice
I have, which you might recall."

Wherever she was going with this,
I didn't want to ask.
We followed the path down to the pond,
where the reflections were almost perfect.

"What was it," Carol asked,
"that Aristotle said about nature—
that in it there is something of…of what?"
I knew the answer but wasn't

sure she'd be pleased if I told her.
Nearby, a few children
were swinging on a jungle gym.
How cleverly they kept figuring out

the best ways not to fall.
We watched them for a while,
and I was aware I was turning
their game into a metaphor

about innocence and understanding.
I suspected Carol was also
running this past her intelligence,
which made me want to surprise

us both by saying something
completely baffling but entirely
true, so Carol would stop and look
at me as if we still shared

a great secret. Those children
were heading home. The water seemed
to be listening. "The marvelous,"
I said, "is what Aristotle believed

is in nature." "Yes," Carol replied,
"that sounds like him. But did he also
think we have to learn
how to be happy?" "Do you?"

"I asked you first." Twilight
emerged from its grove of ash
and elm, reminding us we could leave
if we chose, or stay a little longer.

## WHEN YOU FIND YOURSELF
## REMEMBERING YOURSELF

You've often seen how easily
I can slip away from the moment.
So I'm grateful, really,
that ever since we were girls

you've been trying to save me
from all my impossible thinking.
Isn't it time to admit I'm hopeless?

Yesterday, for example, before
the storm, Frank was helping me
in the garden when the mowers
arrived with their weed-
whackers and leaf-blowers.

"Whatever happened to rakes?"
I said, and Frank agreed
everything in the past
was a lot quieter.

Then I let myself be taken back
to the first house we lived in.

How comforting it felt to fall asleep
to the sound of that little brook
beyond our lawn. How sorry
I was when we moved away.

But things work out
in the end, people say.

Do you believe in signs?
Neither do I. And yet last night
lightning hit so close I knew
our house was gone. I saw

the fire rushing down
from the attic, the wild flames
that might have been real.

Doesn't it mean something—
to be spared?

But you're right. If everything
were a sign we'd never
stop looking. Now tell me—
when you find yourself
remembering yourself,

don't you see someone
dressed up and pretending she's you?
A sun-hat, a new bathing suit,
just the right smile for the occasion?

Because she's young she's hiding
the person she'll be one day.
Of course she doesn't know.

None of us did at her age,
caught up in that great commotion
about the smallest things—

answering the phone one night
or letting it ring.
Deciding what to wear
on a day we couldn't have guessed
might be different from the others.

Later we understand.
Just one of those moments
was enough to turn our lives
into what they've become.

Back then we didn't have a clue.
Which is why it was so lovely.

Or why it seems so now.

# HISTORY

He was never good at it.
Everything kept repeating itself,
one empire disappearing into another,
one ruin the same as the last,

and the people fixed in their importance,
their completed lives.
So he was surprised, opening
the newspaper that morning,

to find a blurred and grainy
picture that could have been
from his high school history
of World War II. Many times

he must have skipped past it
and hardly noticed: a few seagulls
coasting above the horizon,
a battleship sliding through

the gray water, all the sailors
quiet and nervous, and nobody
imagining a moment
as far off as today

in which they'd be remembered
so imprecisely,
lost in a photograph that wasn't
even theirs, as before

they'd been lost in the pages
of a book on a boy's desk—
the smudges of trees in the windows,
and the squeak of chalk

in the distance, while the gulls
dip and soar above the sea
and then are gone, like the dates
of battles, or the death of kings.

# LIES

These are the days of insolence
and denial, which aren't
so different from the other days

when God told us what to do
and we didn't do it,
which meant one plague

after another until finally
God gave up.
He must have decided

we'd never learn, had never
even tried. The lies we believed
we wanted to believe.

The choices we made
returned as history,
then left us with all these

books of predictions and charts
of losses, and the hopes of some
that God might consent

to punish us again, but with one
of those lesser plagues,
so we get to live

and be contrite. This time,
we would tell Him,
we've learned our lesson,

and are very sorry, and will never
do what we did
ever again.

# APRIL AT THE RUINS

## 1

If there's a late spring the plants suffer.

They shouldn't have been
so eager. *Look at you,* I say,

*you almost dead things,*
*bent over, thrown out*
*of the celebration.*

*Just look around and see*
*what you could have been*
*if only you had waited.*

But who speaks
to the flowers these days?

They aren't hiding anything from us.

## 2

In the early morning, frost catches
hold of the new buds that dared
to open. Now, thinks the tree,

I'll have to do this all over,

but next time the leaves will be smaller,
and more vulnerable, and I myself

will be the weaker for it.


3

*Come out, come out* the children beg.
What do they know?


4

That all that we behold is full of blessings?


5

But can this really be
what Wordsworth was thinking
as he hiked around the lakes,
making his way from one ruin to another
in 1798, or five years earlier

when he stood with his sister
beside the same stream, and the wide
expanse of Nature spoke to him,
not as a poet might pretend,
but as he felt it

in the blood,
and along the heart—

6

So what do we have to say for ourselves?

When it's hot the plants suffer.
When it's too wet—they also suffer.


7

Ah Nature,
surely we've betrayed the heart that loved us.

Or to be more precise,
could never love us—

not as we wished to be loved,
as if we were still children

and the world
was trying to touch us.
*Shhhh*

it might be trying to say.

*Once we were children together.*
*Now listen.*

*That time is past.*

5

# SWAN SONG

Plato claimed they sang
most sweetly at the moment

they knew they would die,
though how they knew

he doesn't say. Socrates
had been told the hour

of his death, therefore
the idea appealed to him,

as well it might to anyone
taken by the thought

of shrugging off the body's
weight, then calmly floating

upward through the lucid air.
But death was different

in the days of the gods,
and wisdom as well,

when those who were wise
were also unafraid,

having heard the music
of departure and release.

How free they must have felt.
And yet how easily

loveliness allows us to believe
whatever we want to believe.

## "THE WORLD PROVIDES EVIDENCE
## FOR ALMOST ANYTHING."
### —Tony Hoagland

Sometimes beauty, you said,
is an anesthetic. That morning
ponderous clouds were all
there was of the sky. I watched
their dull progression and felt
what I'd expected to feel

reading your obituary. Sadness,
of course, which isn't the right word,
or the wrong one either—
like that small hesitation
in a poem before nature enters
to be suggestive. Or in a better poem:

when we're asked to think harder.
But right now I just want
the cherry tree in your yard,
the one that keeps throwing
its blossoms away with such abandon.
And I want the drowsy mumbling

of bees, and later the surprise
of stars turning into books
on a high shelf. After which the moon
rises from the sea like a bronze shield
in an ancient story about voyages
and battles, love and tribulation—a story

in which death is capable of grandeur,
or once was, but still should be more
than absence. Should be an arrow
driven through that shield into the heart.
Should be that body grasping its sword
and for a moment refusing to fall.

# GOD CONSIDERS HIS LOSSES

Terror, awe, amazement—
these are the effects
I've always preferred,
like suspending a fiery sword
in the sky, or producing an angel
with something important to say.
How enthralling it was!
How undeniable.
But the men and women
I made out of dust refused
to admit their freedom
required obedience.
They wanted too much.
They wanted to be like me.
So I punished them, so they went on
inventing one false god
after another, burdening
themselves with need,
wasting their devotion on illusion.
They should have been content
to remain as children
and worship me.
Didn't they understand
I wanted to love them?
And yet the world changes
in ways I could have predicted,
but didn't, although I knew
I would finally
disappear from their lives.
After all, I knew everything.

But I let my art
deceive me—the splendor
of an angel's wings
unfolding in the darkness,
and someone like yourself
waking into this vision, baffled
at first, then overwhelmed
by all that glorious and fearful light.

# THE NEXT MOMENT

As soon as I woke up I could tell
it would be wise to stay away
from other people for a while.

Sit on the porch by yourself,
I said to myself. Be someone
alone beside the ocean, trying

to figure out what allows us
to accept the way everything
that's here keeps floating off

into everything that's over.
Then the sparrows,
bathing in the dust

of the dry grass, rise together.
And the white triangles
of sails in the distance

catch hold of the breeze,
as if they had found
their purpose, and might suggest

to a man staring out at the sea
that the next moment
will ask him to wonder

only about the light
on the water, or the sweetness
he can't name

flowering nearby,
and so release him
from whatever fastens his mind

to the day after this one.
And hangs those little weights
from his heart.

# UNTIL EVENING

Repeating themselves, the seasons
become, each year, more symbolic.

In the winter there are huge piles of snow.
In the summer: water lilies.

Summer ends and returns.
We ourselves return, and even if

this hillside conceals another
we might travel to, in the distance

a mountain rises with its sharp peaks
and icy ridges, now impassible.

Of course you're tired.
We're both tired. We should let

the snow accumulate, make a fire,
forget about the shovels by the door.

And if it were summer
we could sit quietly by the pond,

watching the water lilies—
how they don't change,

although if we stayed long enough,
if we waited until evening,

and then the end of evening,
we might see them shiver and close.

# HOMETOWN

Best to begin with Main Street—
our one barbershop, one good bakery,
then that solitary school on its hilltop
above the train station where someone

I know by name will accept my ticket
if I decide to leave. This is the town
most of us have lived in
forever without worrying
if we should live somewhere else,

or should want to. But why,
you might ask, did we allow our elms,
the ones that looked like they still
had a chance, to be taken away?

Why permit that fine old station
to fall into ruin?—doors split,
water staining the marble columns,
as if each new traveler had to see,
as you've seen, what happens

to anything we assume
we don't need. How permanent
our carelessness turned out to be.
After the mills failed,

some of us left. You'd have left
—wouldn't you?—long before.
But now the water's clear. People
fish. And the forsythia's just out,
a brighter gold than I've ever seen.

If you have the time you might
enjoy a walk along the river.
The best way is down that hill
beyond our fancy new hospital.

Yes, it's ugly. I don't know why
they couldn't have done better.
Or why every time I'm there
I wait even longer to be told
what is or isn't wrong. I've learned

not to think too far ahead,
to let my mind slip outside
and look for a better place—
maybe a garden where bumblebees

are going about their business,
and a few women
kneel among the flowers, chatting
and weeding, one of them brushing
her hair back when the breeze

unloosens it. I don't pity us
and you shouldn't either.
In the school the children
are adding and subtracting, but soon

that part of their day will be over.
And as they leave they'll be laughing,
telling each other jokes and secrets,
and singing about what they purely
love to hear—nonsense, isn't it?—

stepping on a crack, falling off a wall
so hard all the king's horses
and all the king's men can never
put you back together again.

# IN AMERICA

Even these days I can sense it—
the old allure of nature, as sweet
and impermanent as winter's first snow.
Or the brilliance of the pear tree
flowering. Or that disc of sun
on water, drifting away from itself,

then back, briefly restored. Once
it was possible to mistake
silence for sympathy. And no one
worried about where nature
was going. Or what would happen
when it got there. Moment by moment

is how children move through the day,
and if in fact they don't I still
want to see them out in the evening
on the darkening lawns, released
from thought. My friend Eric tells me
that to an unencumbered mind

the acceptance of death is freedom.
"Equanimity," he writes,
"has become my dear companion."
I believe him, I believe he's sure of it.
But nostalgia often takes me
back to a time when we might

have invented a better place to live
than where we live now. America,
you were so eager and in love
with yourself—how can we
claim to be surprised
that our grandfather's fathers,

overwhelmed by your endlessness,
decided everything was theirs
to take, and name, and keep?
So they did, and taught us
that anyone who stands in the way
should have known better.

That suffering is the cost of progress.
That we are what we own.
It's not difficult now to confess
their sins and be burdened
by almost nothing, even granted
permission to congratulate ourselves

on our honesty. Quiet concentration
is what Eric says he tries to achieve
without trying. No more
neediness, no more striving.
When I was a kid I was given
a gold star for being good,

and a silver one
for just a little less. How pleased
I was to see them
beside my name on the bulletin board
for the other children
to look at, and envy.

## AT FIRST THEY SEEMED
## LIKE STRANGERS

The rooms kept getting smaller
in the house where I found
myself wandering. Or else this
is how they'd always been,
and memory changed them, allowing
the willows to retreat from our windows,
and the water from the lawn.
As I climbed the stairs I could hear
the others below me.
At first they seemed like strangers,
but soon I knew them—
my parents, sister, friends.
Then they all grew younger,
and for a while
they were content, oblivious
to what time would do to them.
And then they were confused, lost
in the old uncertainties.
And then they were gone,
and the house as well, and I was left
alone in the tall, tangled grass, waiting
as I had when I was a boy
for whatever in my life
was supposed to come next.